Lilibet

AN ACCOUNT IN VERSE
OF THE EARLY YEARS OF
THE QUEEN
UNTIL THE TIME OF HER ACCESSION

BY A LOYAL SUBJECT OF
HER MAJESTY

Blond & Briggs
LIMITED · LONDON

First published in Great Britain in 1984
by Blond & Briggs Limited, Dataday House,
Alexandra Road, London SW19 7JZ

British Library Cataloguing in Publication Data

Loyal Subject
Lilibet.
1. Elizabeth II, *Queen of Great Britain*
2. Great Britain – Kings and rulers – Biography
I. Title
941.085′092′4   DA590

ISBN 0-85634-157-6

Printed in Great Britain by
Butler and Tanner Ltd, Somerset

1926

*M*idnight in *Mayfair*. Hush'd are the dark bricks
In *Bruton Street* of *Number Seventeen*.
Inside, the long-case clock sedately ticks.
Outside, a car draws up, and there is seen
Home Secret'ry, *Sir William Joynson Hicks*.
Softly he enters. Little doth he ween
     That ere the hall clock strikes the hour of three
     A future monarch he is going to see.

Hail to the Princess who, ere break of dawn
Salutes *Sir William* with an infant squawk!
April the Twenty-First, Hail happy morn!
A loyal Empire echoes to the talk.
King George V's first grandchild has been born,
Child to the fair *Elizabeth of York*.
     Sleep on, sweet babe, the sun is shining yet
     Upon thy grandsire's Empire—LILIBET!

In naming thee, Bright Destiny hath shewn
What yet is hid from mortals' sceptic view:
A new *Elizabeth* for *Albion*'s throne;
An *Alexandra*, type of spouse most true.
Her Empress grand-dame next the child would own;
Her third great name outshines the other two:
　　MARY! Celestial Queen and Mother Mild,
　　A worthy Patron for a Royal Child.

1

EARLY CHILDHOOD: GRANDPAPA ENGLAND; THE BIRTH OF PRINCESS MARGARET ROSE

And now, who comes, the royal babe to greet?
The Prince of Wales, her father's elder brother,
Smiles sadly as he drives down Bruton Street:
No wife is his. The heir's born to another.
Queen Mary says, and tweaks the infant feet:
"I wish you look'd more like your little mother."
    And, palely handsome, standing at her side,
    The Duke of York's weak with paternal pride.

"Oh here comes the bambino!" is the cry
Of proud *Queen Mary*, when she comes to call.
"So like the dear *Prince Consort*, though the *eye*
Is *Bertie's image*—there's no doubt at all!!!"
Here is a baby destin'd—who knows why?—
To walk at once, and never choose to crawl:
    Reflecting in her stately head and neck
    VICTORIA and *Princess May of Teck*.

On with my tale! though long a Bard could sit
To pen the infant darling's thousand charms.
Lord Strathmore's house in *Bruton Street* was quit
When LILIBET was still a babe in arms.
The Duke and Duchess took her, as was fit,
To see her "little mother's" house in Glamis:
    The baby gurgled safe inside that house
    While dukes and earls paced out to shoot the grouse.

Another journey, pregnant to recall,
Took place in autumn Nineteen Twenty-Eight,
When the *Bowes-Lyons* rented *Naseby Hall*
To hunt sly *Reynard* and his vixen mate.
And LILIBET could toddle to the stall
And sniff the hay, and eagerly await
  The Duke of York's return, when he, of course,
  Would lift her up and let her pat his horse.

How apt that little LILIBET should bring
To *Glamis* and *Naseby*, dark with Royal curse,
New secret blessing and a Second Spring;
To bleakest hist'ry give a bright reverse:
Great *Glamis*, thou *shalt* hereafter breed a King!
The child who play'd at *Naseby* shall be nurse
  Not to a vanquish'd *Charles*, but one whose fame
  Would win his mother's and his land's acclaim.

At home in *London*, pink with frills and tassels,
The little girl delights in company:
The Honourable George and *Gerald Lascelles*.
Her infant cousins often come to tea.
And share her games as equals, not as vassals;
Loud their delight and gay their glad whoopee,
  As *Katta*, nurs'ry-maid, enchants them all
  By dancing with the dolls as at a Ball.

She's taken to the Palace once a week.
Grandpapa England is the King she's told.
How gruff he sounds when he begins to speak:
Does *England* sound so cross because it's old?
His health is frail: his amply bearded cheek
Must not be kiss'd if one has got a cold.
  One day, he'll die and then they'll have to sing
  God Save *King David*—Uncle will be king.

An old man and an infant on the sand.
His health returns beneath the *Bognor* sky.
For *Grandpapa*, so tweedy, fierce and grand,
Is lov'd by LILIBET and must not die.
Pressing her bucket in his mottled hand,
She lisps, "Please try my sand and apple pie."
  His blue eyes moisten at her playfulness.
  The Emp'ror stoops to kiss the young Princess.

When LILIBET approach'd the age of four,
The house in *Piccadilly* felt a change.
Her lovely mother stay'd at home much more:
"No foreign travel this year." That was strange.
And there were bustlings on the nurs'ry floor,
And *Katta* spoke of "matters to arrange".
  But then, to quieten LILIBET's alarms,
  The household took the train and went to *Glamis*.

15

The sounds of *Glamis*! The piper moaning shrilly,
The bark of dogs in cobbled stable court;
The broad Scotch laughter of a highland ghillie,
Sharing a joke with uncles about sport.
How fresh the air is after *Piccadilly*!
How long the rain-soak'd days, the nights how short!
  The Duke of York relaxes with his gun;
  How sad the Duchess cannot share the fun.

The Princess knows by now the happy cause
That keeps her mother from the grouse and heather:
All day behind those sturdy bedroom doors,
The midwives and the *Duchess* are together.
By evening, the rain no longer pours:
A scarlet sunset and a change of weather.
  An Empire's sunset, grand and gorgeous, glows
  Around the birth of little *Marg'ret Rose*.

2
145 PICCADILLY:
"CRAWFIE"

*H*ow fast the years of childhood onward sped.
The days of babyhood are now no more.
A governess was coming, it was said,
With references from *Admiral Leveson-Gower.*★
When LILIBET first saw *Miss Crawford's* head
Fram'd with an *Eton* crop poke round the door,
    The infant's eyes transfix'd her with a stare,
    And then she ask'd, "Why do you have no hair?"

"Driving in bed?" *Miss Crawford* then complains.
How straight and pink the young equestrian sits!
"Not sleeping yet, in spite of *Alah's* pains?"
The bed's a carriage, and its posts the bits,
Cords of a dressing-gown make up the reins.
"Twice round the *Park* and homewards past the *Ritz*;
    Always I drive thus nightly," she replies.
    "My horses need their daily exercise."

★Pronounced *Looson-Gor.*

At six years old, whenever she was able,
She groom'd her thirty horses, water'd, fed;
Fix'd and remov'd their bridles; brush'd their sable,
Comb'd ev'ry tail and patted every head.
The nurs'ry landing was their airy stable:
They ran on wheels wherever they were led.
    And *Crawfie*, too, to please the little groom,
      With bit and reins would canter round the room.

Sometimes, with noses press'd against the glass,
Down into *Piccadilly* they would stare:
Two rain-drench'd weary drays might sometimes pass
Or coster's pony, dazzl'd by the glare:
Or dairy horses, weighed with straps and brass
Would sadly clip-clop through the foggy air.
    Then LILIBET would sigh and think with pity
      Of all the hard-work'd horses in that city.

"*Crawfie*," she said, "if I am ever Queen,
"I will protect the dobbin and the dray.
"No working horse on Sunday will be seen:
"Horses, like men, deserve a Sabbath day.
"Docking a pony's tail is cruel and mean.
"That will be outlaw'd. Hearken what I say."
    And *Crawfie* smil'd to hear the lisping word;
      The Goddess FORTUNE also smil'd—and heard.

O *Piccadilly* days, why need they end?
The walks with *Crawfie* in *St James's Park*:
Sometimes an eye would turn, a head would bend,
But oftentimes each outing, game or lark
Would pass unnoticed; LILIBET could spend
Her shilling's pocket-money without mark
    From shopkeeper, or children in the street,
    The thousands she could never hope to meet.

Plain *London Transport* was a cherish'd toy:
A 'bus ride—top floor—was the merriest lark.
"*Tott'nham Court Road*. A single." Oh, what joy
To say those brave words to a booking clerk.
And whizz, like any other girl or boy
From place to place by railway in the dark.
    Dear transitory joys, too soon curtail'd
    When cameramen the young princesses trail'd.

More than to most, the growing *Princess* hooks
Her heart to *Uncle David, Prince of Wales*.
His sense of fun; his wonderful good looks,
His jokes, his clothes, his funny trav'llers-tales.
Yet, as he reads aloud her fav'rite books:
Black Beauty, A. A. Milne—his laughter fails:
    A soldier's life is terrible hard, says Alice.
    More than the Guard is changing at the Palace.

3
THE DEATH OF
KING GEORGE V

*I*n *Windsor*, at *The Royal Lodge*, the word
Arriv'd by telegram one winter day.
Alone with her toy horses when she heard,
LILIBET paus'd: "Oh, *Crawfie*, *should* we play?"
She sens'd a mighty passing had occur'd:
With dignity, she put her toys away.
    Marg'ret play'd noughts and crosses in the hall.
    The wireless crackled the Dead March from *Saul*.

4
ABDICATION

*N*othing is restful since *King George* has died.
The servants whisper. *Mummie* looks so sad.
Marg'ret heard *Grannie* talk of "*England's* pride"
And said she heard their father murmur "cad".
Who did it mean, when *Mummie* then replied:
"Not marry her? He must be going mad!"?
    Crawfie had blush'd when ask'd, and sort of frown'd.
    Oh, *when* is *Uncle David* to be crown'd?

One Sunday at *Roy'l Lodge,* uneasy fear
Began to turn to sickening alarm.
A car came over from *Fort Belvedere:*
Out stepped a woman, holding *Uncle's* arm.
But still to LILIBET 'twas far from clear
Why *Mummie,* who was usually so calm,
    Sent the Princesses to the garden's end,
    Lest they should talk to *Uncle David's* friend.

Later, the stricken mother would endeavour
To break the news to her bewilder'd child.
"Your *Uncle David*, usually so clever,
Has been by an *American* beguil'd.
He must away." "Oh, *Mummie*—not forever?"
Bravely, and through her 'flu, the *Duchess* smil'd.
  And while the *Duchess* with her daughter frets,
  Downstairs, the air is thick with cigarettes.

The two princesses hug their poor *Papa*,
Accoutred as an Admiral of the Fleet.
The ashtray smoulders. Out towards the car,
They hear him pacing with uneasy feet.
The morning lingers. Has some evil star
Blighted their lives? They feel too sad to eat.
  Luncheon: The door has opened with a fling.
  LILIBET curtsies to her Lord and King.

Farewell their happy life at 145!
Farewell the schoolroom and the coloured chalk.
The times when "*Grandpa England*" was alive,
And when her father was the *Duke of York*.
Freedom, farewell. No more will she arrive
By 'bus from *Tott'nham* at *St James's Walk*.
  Around the Palace stretch those yards of rail.
  She shudders, as though entering a gaol.

5

THE CORONATION: 1937

*K*ing *George the Sixth* and not *Albert the First*.
To LILIBET, this sounds a little odd.
Papa says that "the boxes" are the worst
Part of the job; the hours that he must nod
Signing and reading; often he has curs'd,
But says that they must give themselves to GOD.
    This thought brings to the drudgery a grace
    Which soon illumines all that gloomy place.

Gloomy indeed *Buckingham Palace* seem'd
After the haunts of girlhood's early days.
The little family had never dream'd
How history would then unfold its ways.
But, when it did, *Hope* in the darkness gleam'd
Down endless corridors cast sunny rays.
    How large it was: yet not without its charms.
    (No private postman could be found at *Glamis*)

Where could the children play? The *King* declar'd
New nurseries would banish all the gloom.
His little girls must not, he said, be scar'd
By all the horrors of *his* childhood room.
Soon to explore the young princesses dar'd.
Their laughter banish'd echoes of the tomb.
    And flunkeys, wall'd a lifetime in that pile,
    Remember'd, after decades, how to smile.

The garden too's a happy pleasure-ground.
A place where they could sport or merrymake.
It echoes to their squabbles and the sound
Of childish innocence: what care they take
To hide wet clothes, and creep indoors unfound
When LILIBET has fallen in the lake.
    Her short brown curls are straight and lank and wet:
    The fault, she yet avers, of *Margaret.*

But, while the girls are ragging on the lawn,
Rehearsals, measurements and preparation
Look forward to the grey but Maytime dawn
Of poor *Papa*'s nerve-racking Coronation.
The family's emotions now are torn
Between regret, joy, panic and elation.
    The girls are thrill'd by all the pomp and glamour;
    But can he take his Oath without a stammer?

In ermine, they are now assembled all:
The coaches wait. *Papa* will soon be seen
In robes of state mysteriously tall.
Bobo makes sure that both the girls have "been".
Torrential rain is splashing in *the Mall*.
Umbrella'd crowds salute their *King* and *Queen*.
> But, while the thousands on the streets are clapping,
> Inside their coach, the little ones are scrapping.

"I hope that *Marg'ret* won't be a disgrace;
Today of all days she must not seem shabby".
So urg'd *Elizabeth*, with anxious face.
She was inclin'd to be a trifle crabby
When trying to put her sister in her place.
Marg'ret was silent in the crowded *Abbey*.
    The tottering peers halloo'd, the choir-boys sang;
    Papa was crown'd by *Cosmo Gordon Lang*.

This is a day to make an Empire proud!
Back at the *Palace* on the balcony
The little girls gaze down upon the crowd.
Mummie is *Queen* and smiling radiantly.
While *Grannie* waves a well-glov'd arm, unbow'd
By all the sadnesses of memory.
    The new *King George*, however strong his nerve is,
    Looks desperately in need of *Senior Service*.

Inside, the guests acknowledge that *Papa* has
Subdu'd an Empire's and a Nation's fears.
From ev'ry Royal House and from as far as
Australia and *Tonga*, they are here.
Swords, coronets and medals and tiaras
Reflect the crystal of th' electrolier.
    And *Uncle Harry*, rather worse for wear,
    Slumps with a glass upon a gilded chair.

She never knew she had so many cousins,
So many *German* princelings of no name,
Who hobble round the corridors in dozens
With dow'ger mothers who all look the same.
She then perceives, amid their aged buzzings,
A fair-hair'd youth and wonders why he came:
    Philip of Greece,'twas said,who'd travelled down
    By overnight express from Gordonstoun.

She star'd a moment at his handsomeness:
Like news-reel pictures of the *Hitler youth*.
Something had stirr'd within the child princess,
Something the years would ripen into truth.
She could not meet him then:the house of *Hesse*
En masse shov'd past her in a horde uncouth.
    And by the time she had her night-dress on,
    And peep'd down from a landing, he was gone.

6
THE LAST MONTHS
OF PEACE: 1939

At *Portsmouth*, come to bid the *King* goodbye,
The girls, with *the Queen Mother*, hide their grief.
Margaret said, "I brought a handkerchief,"
About to dab it to her moistening eye.
But LILIBET's retort was brave and brief.
"Only to wave, dear *Grannie*, not to cry".
    Queen Mary stiffly gave a little frown,
    But later in her diary, wrote it down.

For, in the spring of Nineteen Thirty-Nine,
The King and Queen went to the *U.S.A.*
Back at the Palace, the *Princesses* pine.
They hate it when their parents go away.
But, with reflected glory they can shine
With what the papers and the wireless say.
  The New World loves *the Queen* and, true to form,
  Mummie has taken *Washington* by storm.

For both her daughters, *Mummie's* special charms
Have been a source of purely private pride.
At *Piccadilly*, *Royal Lodge*, and *Glamis*
They've romp'd with her, and learnt to pray and ride.
But now, with loving praise and open arms,
The world salutes her from both far and wide:
  The girls' protectress, model, playmate, chum,
  Has been adopted as the Millions' Mum.

One morning, when the children sat alone,
The Palace telephone began to ring.
"A call by transatlantic telephone".
They heard the voice of *Mummie* and the *King*.
For *Dookie*, the receiver seem'd a bone.
She bark'd a message down the alien thing.
  "Mummie, she *bit Lord Lothian*—such a bore.
  The blood came POURING out on to the floor."

Her mother's laughter is too quickly gone:
Clutching the corgi as the line went dead,
LILIBET wish'd their talk had rambled on;
There were so many things she left unsaid.
She sigh'd and put her *Prussian* chin upon
The top of *Dookie*'s fox-like little head.
  "Don't worry, darling. Though *New York* is far,
  It won't be long before you see *Papa*."

How generous *Mummie* was with all her love!
LILIBET envied all those cheering *Yanks*.
Though *Queen*, she never gaz'd down from above,
Rather brought hope and laughter to the ranks.
Example hard to learn: but time will prove
The *Queen* is worthy of a sad world's thanks.
  "Papa is *King*," thought LIL'BET, "does that mean
  That one day I, like *Mummie*, must be Queen?"

"When he is cross or has his nervous tummy,
Papa says that the job is tears and toil.
'I could not be the *King* without your *Mummie*
So strong, so brave, so Christian, and so loyal'.
One day must I the burden bear—O Lumme—
Alone? O GOD, why *did* you make me royal?"
  She silently commun'd; all *Marg'ret* saw
  Was "*Lil*" and *Dookie* clasp'd upon the floor.

The shadow pass'd, and soon enough, the liner
Brought both her parents home across the main.
Few could recall a summer that was finer,
Nor one more pregnant with despair and pain.
For, wireless sets from *Cheltenham* to *China*
Told how the *Boche* were at their tricks again.
    The anxious *Princess Marg'ret* ask'd the *King*,
    "Who is this *Hitler*, spoiling everything?"

In those last months of Peace, a meeting chanc'd
Which chang'd the Nation's future Destiny.
The Fates conspir'd; not blindly *Cupid* danc'd,
Victoria and Albert cruis'd the sea.
The August sunshine, and fresh wind enhanc'd
The visit of the Royal Family
    To *Dartmouth Naval College*, to perfection
    Drill'd for an expert sailor-King's inspection.

But, as they climb'd the steps, the message came:
"Two boys have mumps. The doctors all advise
The young princesses should not catch the same."
Mummie agreed such caution did seem wise.
Margaret scowl'd. Her sister show'd her shame
At being thought a child, with angry eyes.
    But *Crawfie* took th'indignant "little ones"
    To tea with the *Dalrymple-Hamiltons*.

A clockwork railway on a nurs'ry floor,
Where knelt a handsome boy of eighteen years.
If they had fear'd today would be a bore,
Forgot at once are the *Princesses'* fears.
He stood up when he saw them at the door:
LILIBET felt her eyes had fill'd with tears.

    She wish'd she did not have this silly hat on.
    "We've never met. My name's *Philip Mountbatten*."

At first their greeting was a little staid
But *Philip* soon began his easy quips.
Over the ginger nuts and lemonade,
He told them all they'd need to know of ships.
Then he ask'd LILIBET if she had play'd
Tennis in *his* way. Out she gaily skips
  To watch, then join him in exub'rant sports.
  He leaps the nets and runs about the courts.

"O, *Crawfie*, he can jump so very high!"
LILIBET says before she goes to bed.
Next day, O worthy of a royal sigh,
Another vision of that proud blonde head.
Next day, he came to lunch, and why O why
Did she not write down all he did and said?
  For, deep inside her soul, she feels a peace
  And sighs with longing for *The Prince of Greece*.

On thy dear banks, illustrious *River Dart*,
At thirteen years, fair LILIBET began
To know with certainty within her heart
That she could only truly love one man.
How sad she feels next day when they must part.
Can one so young be sure? *This* princess can.
  "How red she is. I wonder if she's hot",
  The Queen remarks, back on the *Royal Yacht*.

From *Dartmouth* then the *Royal Yacht* sail'd forth,
But not alone, for following in their track,
A host of small boats risk'd a sov'reign's wrath
By bobbing close in many a daring tack.
The King said crossly to *Sir Dudley North*,
"It is absurd—unsafe—they must go back."
    A sharp retort was sent in semaphore,
    And soon the boys were rowing back to shore.

All boys save one: his heart was tied by th' strings
To the majestic rudder on the main.
No ordinance, no order of the *King's*
Could stop him glimpsing LILIBET again.
"Young fool!" *George* stammered. "Boys who do such
       things. . . ."
The sentence died in fury and in pain.
    But, with binoculars around her neck,
    LILIBET gaz'd, till *Philip* was a speck.

7
WAR

With nervous fingers on her necklace coral,
LILIBET hears the dreadful news aghast.
This August, they will *not* go to *Balmoral*,
As they have done for every summer past.
Alas, the *King* and *Queen* both feel a moral
Duty to stay in *London* to the *last*.
     Treats are devised, the hideous blow to soften;
     But *Chamberlain* calls often and more often.

To *Crawfie*, he's a prissy little man.
But *Mummie* says you should not speak like that.
It's not much, but he's doing all he can,
And *Hitler* is a loathsome little rat.
Papa prays GOD to send them all a plan
To keep the peace and not bomb *London* flat.
     Chamberlain's uncle's fact'ry made tin tacks.
     How much they all prefer *Lord Halifax*.

Yet, after very slow deliberation,
The girls were sent to *Scotland* after all.
The private train pull'd out of *King's Cross Station*.
By morning, they can hear the raucous call
Of Scottish porters, see the steep gradation
Of mountain forests and the waterfall.
  LILIBET little guess'd, when in the train,
  That months would pass 'ere she went home again.

Tea is the high point of the day, perhaps:
Back from the grouse moor or their garden strolls,
Hungry for shrimps and toast, bannocks and baps,
The guests assemble. And, hot sausage rolls
Amply precede pre-prandial baths or naps.
White table-cloths—a roaring grate of coals,
  The tartan hangings of the drawing-room.
  VICTORIA breathes an influence from the tomb.

Balmoral's immemorial routine:
The *Crathie* shop with its inflated prices,
Where LILIBET and *Marg'ret*, and the *Queen*
Can go to purchase postcards, stamps and ices;
The cry of curlews; the majestic scene;
Contrive to make them all forget the Crisis.
  But, telegrams insist that they remember.
  The King and *Queen* rush southward in *September*.

WAR was declar'd, and, stable as a rock,
The *Queen* and *King* their watch in *London* keep.
The two princesses feel a sense of shock,
Maroon'd in *Scotland* till the snow is deep.
Mummie rang up each night at six o'clock.
It did not stop them crying in their sleep.
 Salute, my MUSE, brave young ones such as these,
 LILIBET, first of WAR's evacuees!

The months dragg'd by. Evacuees from *Leith*,
And *Glasgow* came to live on the estate.
Poor LILIBET had trouble with her teeth,
And had to wear a painful kind of plate.
Sometimes *Lord Haw-Haw* and sometimes *Lord Reith*
Beguil'd an evening till the hour of eight.
 And *Christmas* shopping for the *King and Queen*
 Was done at *Woolworth's* shop in *Aberdeen*.

For, at the Feast of Yule, they were united;
To *Sandringham* came all the Family.
On *Christmas* Eve, the candles were ignited
As every year upon the *Christmas* Tree.
LILIBET's happiness was largely blighted
By thinking of the *Ark Royal*, lost at sea.
 Yet, joys there were: mince pies, the Guiding Star,
 And being back with *Mummie* and *Papa*.

Simple and brave, direct, yet sadly grand
His wireless message was on *Christmas Day*.
"Go out into the dark, and put your hand
Into the hand of GOD," they heard him say:
Better than light is that upon the land—"
He paus'd—"And safer than a known—er—way."

    And all who heard the broadcast knew one thing:
    GOD had rais'd up a lion-hearted king.

8
WINDSOR

*T*he comforts *Windsor Castle* had were spartan,
And knew an almost daily diminution.
She miss'd *Balmoral* with its jolly tartan,
An altogether friendlier institution.
Here, she was tutor'd by *Sir Henry Marten*,
Who taught her dates and *British Constitution*.
  That *Eton* Provost told her all the facts
  Of guillotines, committees, bills and acts.

And now, for the duration of the War,
At Windsor Castle they must be embower'd!
Her parents stay in *London*, better far
To keep the Heir Apparent close entower'd.
At first, she feels how very cruel they are,
And, entering its courts, feels overpower'd.
  How ghostly *Windsor* is! How like a morgue is
  The atmosphere, unsuitable for corgis.

Mother of *Crackers* and of *Carol, Jane*
Was LIL'BET's fav'rite dog in Nineteen Forty.
In *Windsor Great Park*, picture then her pain,
One day out rabbiting—"Come back, you naughty!"
The corgi ran, and by a car was slain.★
How easy then to weep, or rage, be haughty.
    But LILIBET, without her grief revealing,
    Thought only of the driver and his feeling.

Repeatedly, she told him that the blame,
If blame there were, most surely was her own.
She took the man's—a castle gard'ner's—name,
And wrote to him to comfort and atone.
How many girls would think to do the same?
Small incident, yet one by which is shown
    In LILIBET, the latent quality
    Of roy'l courage and deep charity.

Who would have guess'd, when *Jane* had broken tether
And met her death in that unhappy rush,
How many corgis, added altogether,
That Princess would have own'd? Bomb sirens, hush!
Allow a minstrel to digress of *Heather*,
Tinker and *Foxy, Buzz* and *Sherry, Brush*,
    Susan and *Sugar*, who would be so frisky,
    Shadow and *Smokey, Clipper, Sparky, Whisky.*

★ That short-legg'd run, O *Jane*, created you.
First Royal casualty of World War II.

Look forward to the days, if you are able,
When Peace has triumph'd over wartime's shocks;
When, as the *Queen*, she'll lead forth *Myth* and *Fable*
Or go for walks with *Jolly* or with *Socks*;
While *Piper* growls at *Tiny* 'neath the table,
And shakes the scones, the sandwiches and crocks.
    O happy, full-of-corgis future day,
    From war's deep dark, we gaze towards thy ray!

The *Windsor* Years, the five long *Windsor* years
Saw LILIBET grow up to womanhood.
The shy, self-righteous infant disappears.
The new *Elizabeth* is simply good.
As Girl Guide, she mucks in and volunteers
To scrub the pots and pans and chop the wood.
    Back at the Castle, she as well fits in as
    Hostess at dolls' house as at grown-up dinners.

In velvet boiler suit, the two princesses
Sleep nightly in the dungeons during raids.
By day, in uniform or gingham dresses
They study French or practise for parades,
Or tend allotments; one of them confesses
A secret pride in skill with hoe and spade:
    So, gardeners might glimpse a future *queen*
    Exulting in a crop of fine dwarf bean.

And all admir'd the gay and clever manner,
In *Windsor*, year by year at *Christmas* time,
With jolly tunes play'd out upon the piano,
In which the girls perform'd in pantomime,
Produc'd and organiz'd by *Hubert Tanner*.
The King guffaw'd at every joke and rime:
    Yet on the costumes cast a sterner eye.
    The Heir Apparent must not show her thigh.

Queen Mary smil'd when *Marg'ret* wrote to tell her
The wonderful success that she had had in
The starring role, one year in *Cinderella*.
LILIBET next year play'd the leading lad in
(Principal boy, that is, the *Twankie* fella)
The *Windsor Castle* version of *Aladdin*.

 Backstage, she whisper'd, turning rather pink,
 "Oh *who* has come to see us act, d'you think?"

Her charming *Prince* is there in the front row,
His steely eyes fix'd firmly on the stage:
And no historian can ever know
What tempests in his bosom toss and rage,
As LILIBET, sixteen, tries not to show
The passions nat'ral to that tender age:
> She does not miss a cue. He cries *Encore*!
> For one short hour they can forget the war.

But not for long: the war's continued follies
Have years to run. And my Muse must be *Melp-*
Omene*, while *Philip's* on the *Wallace*,
Later a *First Lieutenant* on the *Whelp*.
For LILIBET, her one continued solace
In private longing, must be all the help
      She gives, with ever growing dedication
      In varied services to KING and Nation.

When LILIBET had liv'd but sixteen years,
The offices of War she must embrace,
As Royal Colonel of the *Grenadiers*:
After the *Duke of Connaught*, who the place
Fill'd of his sainted father, when the tears
Of widowhood ran down VICTORIA's face.
      Thus *Connaught* doth the *Windsor girl* divide
      From *Windsor's Widow* with a single stride.

But on that birthday all her harmless pride
Could not her simple sense of duty change.
The Colonel dress'd herself as a Girl Guide
And register'd herself at the *Exchange*
Of Labour, down in *Windsor*; for the tide
Of war was not diminish'd, nor the strange
      Conviction firmly held by that Princess
      That she should join up with the A.T.S.

*Muse of Tragedy.

A subaltern that *Colonel* chose to be:
To share her countrywomen's slog and toil
In Transport Training down at *Camberley*;
With aching shoulders, fingers black with oil
She chang'd the wheels and handled dext'rously
The sparking plug and the electric coil.
    'Till in her sober khaki battledress,
      The Unit came to love that brave *Princess*.

Thus, driving ambulances, she acquir'd
Both human contact and mechanic skill.
(Even today, *the Monarch*, if requir'd,
Could mend a gasket or a clutch at will.)
But all the while, *King George* was growing tir'd.
LILIBET knew that he was very ill,
    And often, home from *Camberley* quite late
      Would help her father with affairs of State.

Throughout the Blitz, the *King* and *Queen* had borne
The rôle of parents to their people's plight:
Been to the bomb-sites, comforted those torn
By grief or hopelessness in that long fight.
And, sleepless after raids, heard till the dawn
The voices on the wireless ev'ry night:
    The cruel ranting of dictators harsh,
    Or laughter at *Much-Binding-In-The-Marsh*.

Though worn with worry and fatigu'd by pain,
The King his stony path of duty saw:
Learnt all the details of each new campaign
And follow'd all the progress of the war.
Where lesser men in sick-bed would have lain,
He soldier'd on, until a CHRISTIAN law
    Restrain'd each trigger-happy Nazi junker
    And TYRANNY lay vanquish'd in a bunker.

The vict'ry-dizzy crowds mill round to see
Their conqu'ring lords, and jubilantly stare
At all the faces on the balcony:
The King in naval uniform is there;
The Queen, in feathers, waving joyfully;
And *Churchill*, reassuring teddy-bear,
   Weeps at the blessing of his Royal Master
   To think how close the world came to disaster.

They stood there waving down in wistfulness
Eight years before on Coronation Day.
And by her father stood the young Princess,
Smiling, as now, yet in a different way:
The little girl, half thrill'd with fancy dress,
Is grown a woman, uniform'd in grey.
 No doubt can now be voic'd, as then was known,
 About who next would occupy the throne.

9
PHILIP

With Peace, the *King* and *Queen* set to creating
A separate household for the Heir, complete
For all her growing needs and duties, stating
That LILIBET should have a private suite,
A footman and her first lady-in-waiting.
Yet all was quiet, dignified and neat.
　　She had no love of pomp or ostentation,
　　And keenly felt the hardships of her nation.

Little she entertain'd. It caus'd remark,
When, home from sea, *Prince Philip* often came
And drove her much too fast across Hyde Park
To plays or films, or to a polo game.
Bright in his breast still glow'd the hopeful spark
And LILIBET quite clearly felt the same:
　　No doubts her first fond rapture had defil'd.
　　She lov'd him purely and was yet a child.

When *Philip* call'd, no special fuss was made.
All was as simple as a child might wish.
A good plain nurs'ry dinner would be laid;
No indigestible, exotic dish,
No costly wines—a jug of orangeade
Wash'd down the mash'd potato and the fish,
  And then they'd open wide the nurs'ry doors
  And chase and gambol down the corridors.

Electric light-bulbs smash and pictures fall
As he and *Margaret* and LILIBET
Cavort with rackets and with tennis-ball,
Using the heavy curtains as the net.
Their girlish laughter echoes in the hall:
"Love thirty, forty—game and match and set!"
  The Queen smiles sadly at the noise above.
  O Love, O happy, childish, laughing Love!

The voice of rumour buzzes through the land;
A sneering, peering voice, a cruel whine:
"When will he ask for the Princess's hand?"
Her secretary's never off the line.
She keeps her counsel, and with trembling hand
Puts on a song by *Oscar Hammerstein*:
  The gramophone consoles: and when at home, her
  Most favour'd record hit is *Oklahoma*.

SONG: "THE EMPIRE WILL SAY WE'RE IN LOVE"

LILIBET SINGS:

Why won't the horrid papers just leave us both in
    peace?
Why should the Presses clatter with *Philip, Prince of
    Greece*?
We must de-vise a plan, when they say you are my
    man;
Listen to me, a royal decree, of DON'Ts for you:

> 1. Don't always dance with me,
>   Don't try to ring too much.
>   Don't shoot with the King too much:
>   *Crawfie will say we're in love.*
>
> 2. Don't make advance to me:
>   Your great-great-great grandmama
>   Was *Queen Vic*—how grand you are!
>   *Marg'ret will say we're in love.*
>
> 3. Don't start connecting things:
>   We're cousins at three remove.
>   People will start suspecting things.
>   *England will say we're in love.*

71

Reasons for fear and doubt were found in plenty.
Philip was rash and reckless and conceited:
In ev'ry car in which he drove or went, he
Appear'd to speed or crash in scrapes repeated.
And, as for LILIBET, at scarcely twenty,
How could she know her judgement was not heated?
  She'd scarcely ever known another man:
  Should she not have more time to think or plan?

All but the girl herself felt mov'd to speak.
The nation's tittle-tattle caus'd her pain.
Some newspapers had even had the cheek
To tell young LILIBET to think again.
The man was foreign: wasn't he a *Greek*?
No? Just as bad—his father was a *Dane*.
  You'd really think that such a girl as she
  Would choose *an English Lord* who's C of E.

Philip himself, of *English* mother born,
Bred in these shores and serving in our fleet,
Discreetly made arrangements to be shorn
Of foreign name; to make the break complete,
His princedom and his birthright now are gone.
No heir to foreign kingdoms, he can greet
  His lov'd one with a heart that's free and large:
  A loyal subject of the good *King George*.

He chose his mother's surname because her
Great *Uncle Bertie* was an English king;
But could not take the handle *Battenburg*
(Though that was thought a rather better thing
Than *Schleswig-Holstein-Sonderburg-Glucksburg*,
His father's name, which lack'd an *English* ring).
    This whiff of *German* in those days was tricky.
    Mountbatten he'd be call'd, like *Uncle Dickie*.

King George himself, beset by good advice
And all the chatter which disturb'd the nation,
Decided *Philip*, though the man was nice
And good at sport and dinner conversation,
Must prove his love and pay the heavy price
Of an extended time of separation.
    In *Africa*, *George* had a four-month spell;
    The Queen and the *Princesses* went as well.

Torment for LILIBET, this frightful tour,
In *Capetown* heat, with England under snow
(The coldest months for fifty years or more).
O, *why* did she and *Marg'ret* have to go
And shake the hands of *Zulu*, *Jew* and *Boer*?
Sure of her love she was and well did know
    Delay and disappointment could not flatten
    The ardour of *Lieutenant P. Mountbatten*.

Yet, even as she miss'd him, she could prove
Love vain, lov'd she not honour more than him:
Her heart was ever set on things above
The changing chances of mere passion's whim.
She broadcast to the *Empire* that her love
For all its people never would grow dim:
    The day she came of age, she told her dream;
    With strength expounded the Imperial Theme.

She spoke in accents clear to ev'ry nation:
Young words a weary world design'd to rouse.
She formally declar'd her dedication,
And to her father's rod of *Empire* bows.
Who doubts it was a heaven-sent vocation?
She said: "GOD help me to make good my vows.
   "And those who share my resolution, too,
   "I pray ALMIGHTY GOD bless all of you."

Did some ship's wireless those great words relay
To *Philip* on the other side of earth?
Who knows? The world itself had heard that day
What patience, service, fortitude were worth.
At length, the *Vanguard* sail'd from *Table Bay*.
The seas roll'd onwards to a newer birth.
   And every mile the *Vanguard* sail'd the sea
   LILIBET's heart grew lighter and more free.

Two months would pass before they were betroth'd;
But let us not ask how those months were spent.
They were together. How they must have loath'd
The fact that gossipping would not relent;
Until those words, in formal cover cloth'd,
"*The King has gladly given His consent
   "This tenth day of July in '47*",
Offer *Prince Philip* a foretaste of Heaven.

10
THE OPTIMISTS

From *Bruton Street*, a score of years ago,
An infant *Princess* did an Empire greet:
And now, from *Norman Hartnell*'s studio
Comes forth a wedding-dress from *Bruton Street*.
In *Duchesse* satin, white as driven snow,
Pearls on embroider'd tulle, and roses sweet.
    A coupon-weary nation at this sight
    Gasps with amazement and a pure delight.

The Day has dawn'd! The bells have rung and rung;
The all-night watchers on the pavements drowse.
Now LILIBET, so innocent and young,
Stands at the altar steps to make her vows.
The Scottish air of *Crimond* then is sung
And *Philip, Duke of Edinburgh*, bows
    To *Queen* and *King* before, with simple charm,
    He takes his Princess on his steady arm.

The heart of old *Queen Mary* nearly cracks
When the bride curtsies to the *King*, and while
Trumpets play fanfares by *Sir Arnold Bax*,
The bride and groom move slowly down the aisle.
LILIBET's lovely features can relax
Into a nervous, self-effacing smile.
      The crowds are cheering as they see them pass,
      Gliding like magic in the coach of glass.

The whole day passes like a Fairy Tale.
For every crown'd and uncrown'd head is here.
The toasts are stutter'd out: but O, how pale
And drawn and worried does *the King* appear!
And when she kisses him goodbye, how frail
His sad embrace, and in his eyes what fear!
      Then off to honeymoon via *Waterloo*,
      Crackers was waiting in the landau too.

Dear *Lord Mountbatten*, clever brave and kind
Had lent them *Broadlands* for the honeymoon.
In coming years, they both will come to find
His sane advice and wit a cherish'd boon.
How great their love! How very much they mind—
Their secret days together end so soon.
    The joy and solace of the new young wife
    Must be exchang'd for work and Public Life.

In *Windlesham* they liv'd, until the state
Of *Clarence House* had undergone repair.
The Duke had no more than a year to wait
Before *the Princess* gave birth to an heir.
And in *November Nineteen forty-eight*
(With no Home Secretary standing there)
    LILIBET, in a bed hung round with chintz,
    Safely gave birth unto an infant *Prince*.

Only twelve years before, The Abdication
Threaten'd the future of the *Monarchy*.
But now is born another generation,
Bringing a sense of strong security
To *Crown*, to *Commonwealth* and to the *Nation*.
The baby shows forth, unequivoc'lly,
    However black its former faults or sins are,
    There is a future for the *House of Windsor*.

The adulation and the public joy
Make of this peaceful birth a grand event.
For LILIBET, the handsome little boy
Has brought into her heart a deep content,
Which even *the King*'s illness can't destroy.
And happy, private hours with *Charles* are spent.
    Margaret loves him too, although she can't
    Enjoy the appellation, *Charley's Aunt*.

The birth of *Anne Elizabeth Louise*
Also brought great rejoicing to the land.
That very day, *Prince Philip* on the seas
Had been gazetted to his own command.
He could have taken higher rank with ease;
For years of naval service he had plann'd.
    But, as *the King* grew iller, time grew short.
    How brief, however, *Philip* never thought.

At home, they lov'd the growing little imps.
Abroad, when *Philip*'s ship was dock'd in *Malta*,
Of private happiness they caught a glimpse:
His love of polo did not change or falter.
Against his *Uncle Dickie*'s team, *The Shrimps*,
He scor'd a goal and yank'd the pony's halter.
    LILIBET proudly watch'd him in the lists;
    And *Philip*'s team was call'd *The Optimists*.

The King's decline meant *Philip* could not stay
In his command of *Magpie* on the seas.
"I think *the Duke of Windsor* to us'd say,
When times were bad—'O, anything to please'."
A silent valet caref'lly pack'd away
His spear-guns, uniforms and water-skis.
    He quipp'd, but not without a look of pain:
    "I don't suppose I'll need those things again."

11
OFFICIAL DUTIES 1951

Turn back the albums and the picture-books:
The Trooping of the Colour '51.
How ev'ry inch a future Queen she looks,
Upright on *Winston*, clopping one by one
Past guardsmen. She no kind of slackness brooks;
As though she saw each medal, sword and gun;
    As though *King George the Fifth*'s exacting eye
    Fell on the soldiers as that girl rode by.

And some there were astonish'd by the rigour
And firmness of the Trooping that she made.
Yet, something in that stiff and scarlet figure,
Riding alone around *Horseguards' Parade*,
Made ev'ry heart aware of something bigger
Than music, bear-skin, helmet, coat or braid:
    Even as when the standard was unfurl'd,
    They glimps'd a kingdom not of this bad world.

Tir'd by disease, and war, and deprivation,
The world receives her as a novelty.
A perfect image for a jaded nation
Who seeks again its vanish'd sense of duty:
A *Princess* whose unflinching dedication
Shines forth in fresh-complexion'd child-like beauty.
    So, as *The King* declines into the grave,
    They look to LILIBET to guide and save.

A simple truth upon the world has burst,
That sees her in *The Mall* upon her cob:
So pois'd, so strong, so perfectly rehears'd,
She rides in state before the awe-struck mob:
That never, since *Elizabeth the First*
Was born a monarch so good at her job.
    This ride of dignity makes clear to all
    ELIZABETH will be professional.

The Duke and she must often represent
Her royal father in their foreign tours.
In autumn Nineteen fifty-one they went
On his behalf to far *Atlantic* shores,
To hear the sound of that great Continent
Where *New York* traffic and *Niagra* roars;
    Both *Canada*, of Commonwealth a part,
    And the U.S. take *Philip* to their heart.

They went to *Washington*: like ev'ry where,
A place where they were both at once respected.
President Truman lov'd the Royal Pair,
So young, so friendly and so unaffected.
They met his mother, who was heard declare:
"Honey, I'm thrill'd your father's re-elected."
    But soon they learnt that this meant nothing sinister.
    Churchill had been return'd as The Prime Minister.

How sad young parents had to be away
For *Charles's* birthday, and to be instead
Waving at crowds of strangers on *Broadway*.
"He's so like dear *Prince Albert*," *Grannie* said.
When they got back, *The King* look'd worn and grey,
And had to spend half of each day in bed.
      LILIBET found the path of duty stern.
      Charles hardly greeted her on her return.

Australia's the next place on the list:
New Zealand and *East Africa* as well.
Though these commitments could not be dismiss'd,
Being away from *Charles* and *Anne* was hell.
Yet, chance of holiday could not be miss'd,
And they agreed to have a little spell
      In which official duties they could dodge;
      Kenyan vacation at Sagana Lodge.

King George the Sixth was coughing badly—very.
Doctors suggested *Durban* for the sun.
He'd take young *Peter Townsend*, that equerry
Whom *Margaret* found such terrific fun.
Christmas in *London* wasn't all that merry.
It lack'd the gusto of a *Norfolk* one.
      Sandringham: every *Christmas* in the past
      Was spent there by *King George*, except his last.

Lilibet felt unease. It was horrific
To know that one day soon *The King* would die.
He took them, their last week, to *South Pacific*,
And "Some Enchanted Ev'ning" made them cry.
But, next day, at the airport, no specific
Meaning seem'd fix'd to his subdu'd goodbye.
    The 'plane was there. LILIBET clamber'd on.
    He wav'd his last weak wave, and she was gone.

12

FEBRUARY 5TH–6TH, 1952

At *Sandringham*, the *King* is shooting hare.
The beaters follow, anxious not to lag.
Beneath a large blue sky, he breathes crisp air;
Nor do his energies appear to flag.
The company was good, the sport was fair:
Two hundred hares and eighty were the bag.
    How cold and stiff the rows of corpses are;
    He shivers as he strolls back to the car.

Dinner as usual; and his weary face
Beneath the glare of the electric light
Is animated as, soon after grace,
He tells of how he got a left and right.
Then, tiring, he sinks back into his place
And acquiesces in an early night.
    One final cigarette. "Goodnight", he said,
    And went to drink his chocolate in bed.

Goodnight, sweet Prince! The earth rolls on to dawn.
While from your shoulders slumber lifts the load
Which you, with hardship, have so bravely borne.
Go out into the dark upon that road,
O CHRISTIAN soul! which leads to *God*'s bright morn.
 The earthly sun is gone, but by and by
 Will rise and blazon in the *Kenya* sky.

It glistens now on the *Sagana* Water,
And penetrates the woods of *Aberdare*,
Where stirs the dying *King*'s beloved daughter
To taste the freshness of the morning air.
And all *the King* had, by example, taught her
Is needed by that waking Princess there.
 Where is thy bitterness and sting, O DEATH?
 Arise, unheeding, QUEEN ELIZABETH!

Treetops Hotel, and from a balcony,
Binoculars train'd on the water-buck,
She talks to friends of fishing; playfully
Boasting of catch that day. "Beginner's luck".
No one replies. *Philip* approaches. He
Seems oddly silent. He's not often stuck
 For words. His face is drawn with silent gloom.
 He takes her arm and leads her to her room.

94

FINIS

NOTE

The Author has contrived to make LILIBET as little as possible a work of the Fancy, and is indebted to the following books, to which reference has been made in the course of the Poem's composition:

Marion Crawford: *The Little Princesses* (1950)
Graham and Heather Fisher: *The Crown and the Ring* (1972)
Robert Lacey: *Majesty* (1977)
Keith Middlemas: *The Life and Times of George VI* (1974)
Dermot Morrah: *To be a King* (1968)
L. A. Nickolls: *The Reign of Elizabeth II* (1952)
James Pope-Hennessy: *Queen Mary* (1959)
Anne Ring: *The Story of Princess Elizabeth* (1930)
Betty Spencer Shew: *Royal Wedding* (1947)
Sir John W. Wheeler-Bennett: *King George VI, His Life and Reign*
Godfrey Winn: *The Young Queen* (1952)
Louis Wulff: *Queen of Tomorrow* (1946)
Louis Wulff: *Elizabeth and Philip* (1947)

The Author is also, and most chiefly, indebted to the Private Secretary of Her Majesty the Queen for supplying information.